Goodnight
the Book

Text Copyright © 2018 Tahlonna Grant
Illustrations Copyright © 2018 The Secret Art Gallery
All rights reserved.

ISBN: 0692259236
ISBN-13: 978-0692259238

All rights reserved. No part of this book may be reproduced or transmitted in any form or by any means, electronic or mechanical, including photocopying, recording, or by any information storage or retrieval system, without permission in writing from the publisher.

PRINTED IN USA

www.goodnightthebook.com

Written by
Tahlonna Grant

Illustrated by
Leeron Morraes

GOODNIGHT TOKYO pg 10

GOODNIGHT NEW YORK pg 12

GOODNIGHT MIAMI pg 14

GOODNIGHT RAYVILLE pg 16

GOODNIGHT LONDON pg 18

GOODNIGHT SEATTLE pg 20

GOODNIGHT HONG KONG pg 22

GOODNIGHT ORLANDO pg 24

GOODNIGHT LAS VEGAS pg 26

GOODNIGHT SYDNEY pg 28

GOODNIGHT SAN FRANCISCO pg 30

GOODNIGHT JACKSONVILLE pg 32

GOODNIGHT YOSEMITE pg 34

GOODNIGHT BIG SUR pg 36

BONUS GOODNIGHTS pg 38

good night Tokyo

Goodnight Tokyo, city of racing at night
Where skyscrapers abound
And couples dance in the light
Colorful lights are all I see
At night.

Bright signs all about
That tell me nothing and only leave doubt
A place full of signs and mystery
Where the parks are a plenty
And the lakes are a many
In a city known
For its tall buildings.

Cherry blossom trees canopy us.
Thousands of trees
For you and me to see
Waiting and watching
For us to grow
In this magnificent glow,

                Goodnight Tokyo.

good night New York

A cotton candy cloud
made of sugar
Brooklyn bakery always
Kneading bread for the neighborhood
A lady and a man
both wearing black
happen to end up in
the sugar cloud
They aren't wearing
all black anymore!
He kisses her
the sugar scatters
all around them--
A sugarcloud!
They laugh
the bubble pops
she screams
he smiles.

good night Miami

The city of sparkling lights
that shine oh-so-bright!
A place where one can swim
even when its dim--

Bay, beach, or waterway
Pick your perfect place
to play the day away!

Or maybe you'd just like
to sit by the pool,
and sip on something cool,
Perhaps out of a coconut?

good night Rayville

A tiny town
stuck in another time
Things move slow
People have few places to go
Except Monroe.
I've never been
But heard about it from a friend
Who last went when he was ten.
Long, lazy summers with only two
stoplights in town
He marveled at the closeness of the families
even when the crops were brown.

good night London

The night is wet and cold
She pulls her trench coat
tightly around her
Little cars zoom by
      CAUGHT
in the halo of light.
She looks behind her
The eye stares back
She zooms away
An unlikely speed racer
      CAUGHT
in the snapshot of a London night.

Goodnight Seattle

Summers in Seattle
Nothing better
Beats the weather
Crisp cool air
Cotton clouds and lake houses
Boats
Sailing by
The space needle spins
In a city without a twin
Known for its frequent rain
Cold, overcast and gloomy
They say
unless they've stood in the sun
on a Seattle summer day!

                  Goodnight, Seattle.

good night Hong Kong

It's the year of the fire Chicken,
Red lanterns dangle
Lions and dragons dance in the packed streets
Red envelopes are given
"Hongbao!" scream the excited children--
It's Chinese New Year!

Bright, colorful costumes of red and gold,
Parade floats dance by
Drums and cymbals bang
Music into the ear--
It's Chinese New Year!

The Lantern Festival ends it all
A week of celebrations
Saying goodbye to Fall
Fireworks crackle and delight
As the Pearl of the Orient
says "Goodnight."
        Good night, Hong Kong.

goodnight Orlando

Orlando
The city of oranges
Sitting in the center of the state
Surrounded by a chain of lakes
Summertime brings daily showers
Even after the flowers
As the rain clears
The inevitable steam appears
You know exactly what I mean
If you've been on the Orlando Scene
Theme parks and play places
Dominate the spaces all around
Luckily the grownups still have downtown.
                         Goodnight, Orlando.

good night Las Vegas

The desert is a strange place
So quiet at night
Yet the wind still speaks
Hot and firm
Dry and persistent
The wind moves you
It howls at you day and night

The desert palms sway
Gently in the breeze
To the familiar wind's song
It finds you and asks
Are you coming or going?

The machines jingle
And the people tingle
But wonder why
Their pockets are always dry

People
Constantly moving
In and out
Of this city of contrasts
Dark yet bright
Illuminated in the sparkling light
Will you stay another night?

good night Sydney

Sparkling blue waters
as deep as a spring sky
Boats buoy in the harbor
Just waiting to say 'Hi'
When the skyline beckons
You listen to its call
And lay back and wonder
How such immense beauty
can make you feel so small.
Beautiful pink sand beaches
beckon you
to stay and play
on a warm sunny lovely
Aussie day.

good night San Francisco

Sidewalk cafes
Tall trees -- redwoods
Cozy smells
Wood-burning fireplaces
The evening fog rolls in
A sip of a warm, frothy drink
A bright red trolley
Whistles by
And she shivers a little
From the cold wet spray
Coming off the San Francisco Bay.

goodnight Jacksonville

Jacksonville, how I love you
Why I love you
Only I know
And those that love you also

River city, the First Coast
As you are known
Curious creeks, lazy lakes, connecting
Canals
Create
A space at medium pace

Slow but fast
Here we don't worry about the past
We'd rather sit on the beach and have
a blast
Blankets pulled tight we
Snuggle in our homes
And love the fact that we
never feel alone

                Goodnight Jacksonville

good night Yosemite

Woods abound on a cold
snowy night
A place where one can find
a mountain lion
Crossing into the light
Trees on both sides
Everywhere you go
Leading the way
to perhaps a place you don't know
Feels that way
When you're deep

In woods thickened by
snow sheets
until suddenly
A shooting star
Comes down
and starts to glow
And then you realize
Actually
this place is
Somewhere
that I do know!

good night Big Sur

Twisty turny roads
Mountains on both sides
Where cliffs abode
Calling you to the edge
With its gentle whisper
'Whooosh' says the waves
'Come here' says the apparition
And before you know it
You're standing on the edge
Of a cliff
Looking behind you
Not wanting to look down
So so high up
Higher than the eagles fly
But you're not a bird
So you step back
And enjoy the view
From wherever you are.

Bonus: Goodnight paintings

and to you we say goodnight...

about the author

If you are reading this, you picked up my book. And you opened it. And turned some pages to get here. For that, I thank you. My greatest joy is sharing my poetry and stories with people just like you.

Tahlonna Grant is a writer, educator, and publisher. She is the author of Goodnight the Book and The Adventures of Scooter and Lima Bean series.

For more information and extension activities, please visit www.goodnightthebook.com.

The illustrator was born in Singapore. He was taught by his mom to draw when he was two. And at five, a robot showed him the secrets. Find out more @ TheSecretArtGallery.com

www.beansproutbooks.com